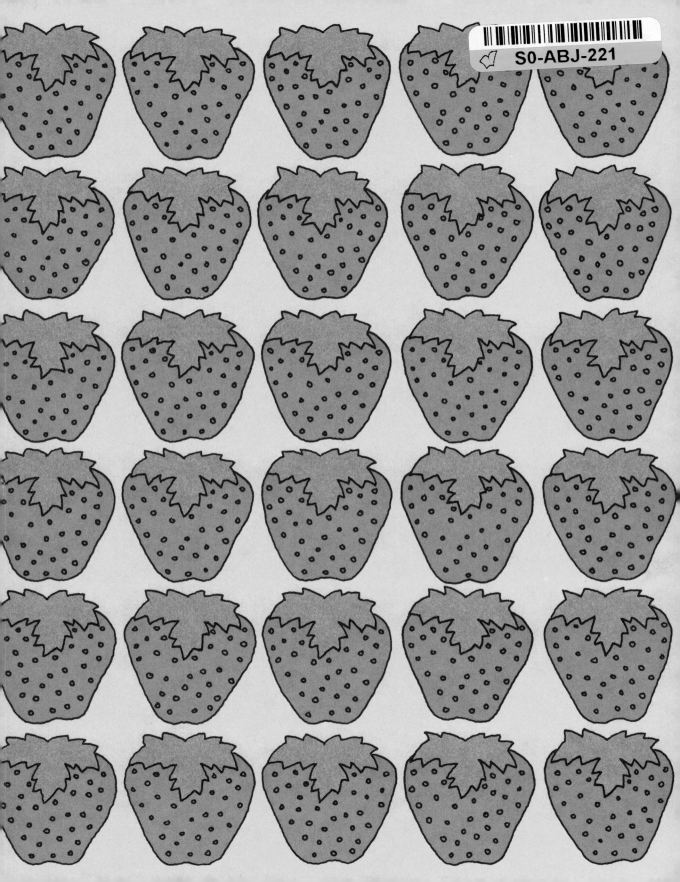

this
strawberry book
belongs to

this book
is for
Tess
and
Walter

the strawberry
picture
dictionary

by Richard Hefter

a strawberry book®

a A

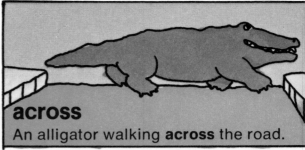

across
An alligator walking **across** the road.

above
An apple **above** an alligator.

about
This book is **about** words.

actor
An **actor acting**.

accident
An alligator **accident**.

add
An alligator **adding**.

adult
A grown-up.

acrobat

afraid
This alligator is **afraid** of an ant.

again
An actor acting **again**.

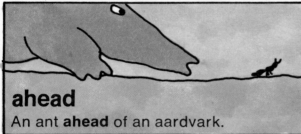

ahead
An ant **ahead** of an aardvark.

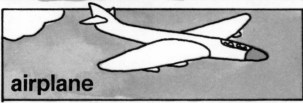

airplane

alone
An alligator **alone**.

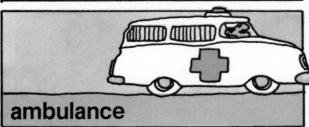

ambulance

anchor

angry
Angry animals.

another
Another alligator accident.

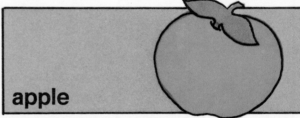

apple

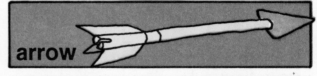

arrow

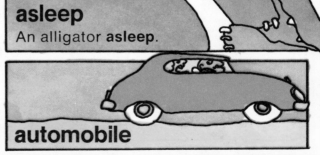

asleep
An alligator **asleep**.

automobile

axe

b B

baby

bag

ball — football, basketball, baseball

balloon

banana

barber
A bear at the **barber's**.

barn

basket
A bear in a **basket**.

bath
A bear in a **bathtub**, taking a **bath**.

bed
A bear in **bed**.

behind
A bear **behind** a box.

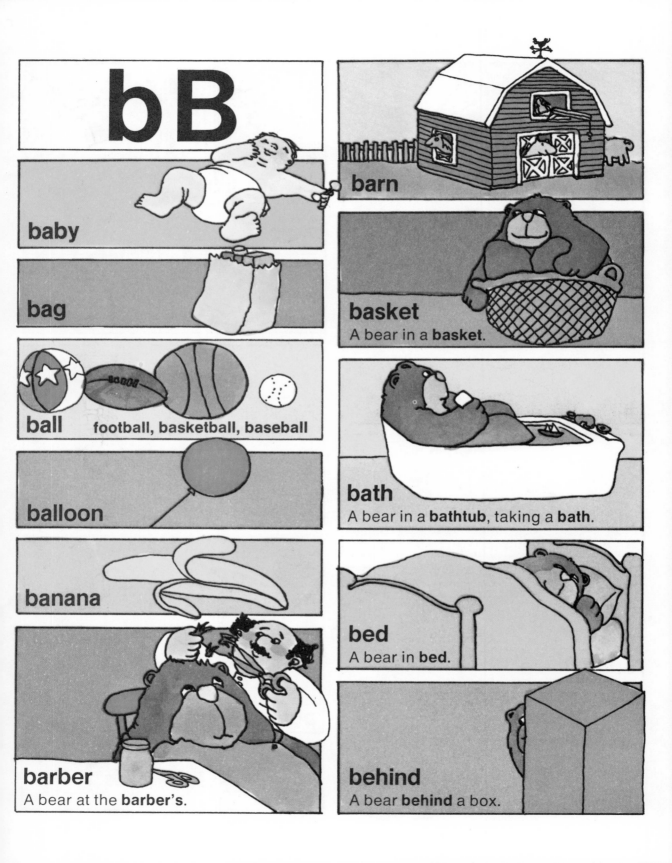

beside
A bear **beside** a box.

between
A bear **between** two boxes.

bicycle

big
Big bear, **bigger** bear, **biggest** bear.

bird

birthday
"Happy **birthday**, Bear!"

boat

book

boot

bridge

bump

bus

c C

candy

cage
A cat in a **cage**.

car

cake

catch
A cat **catching** cans.
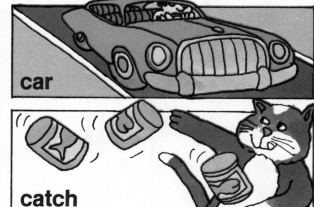

calf
A baby cow.

chair

can
This cat **can't** open a **can**.

chase
A chicken **chasing** a cat.

cheese

This cat **can**.

chin

climb

A cat **climbing** a chimney.

clock
ticktock

coat

A clown in a **coat**.

corn

cry

The clown is **crying**.

d D

dark

A dog in the **dark**.

deep

A duck in **deep** water.

dentist
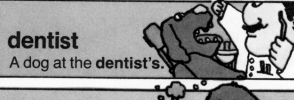
A dog at the **dentist's**.

dishes

Doing dirty **dishes**.

doctor
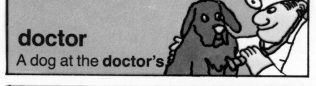
A dog at the **doctor's**

door
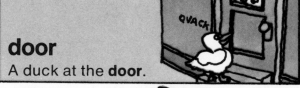
A duck at the **door**.

down
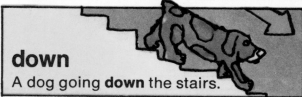
A dog going **down** the stairs.

drink

A dog **drinking**.

drum

e E

ear

eat
An elephant **eating** eggs.

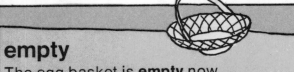

empty
The egg basket is **empty** now.

entrance
In.

eye

exit
Out.
Elephants **exit** here.

f F

face
A fox **face**.

fall
A fox **falling**.

family
Father Fox and his **family**.

far
The fox is **far** away.

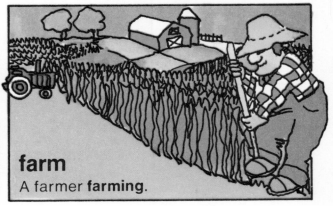

farm
A farmer **farming**.

fast
A **fast** fox.

fat
A **fat** fox.

feet
Fox **feet**. A man's **foot**.

fence
A fox on a **fence**.

fire
Fire fighters fight **fires**.

first
The **first** fox in line.

five
Five fingers.

fix
Can you **fix** a flat tire?

flag

fly
Birds **fly**.

food

friend
A frog and his **friend**.

frown

g G

game
These goats are playing a **game**.

garbage

The **garbage** collector loads **garbage** onto a **garbage** truck.

garden

gasoline

The **gasoline** pump is empty.

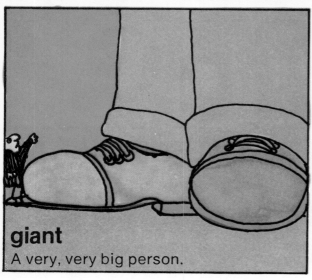

giant

A very, very big person.

giraffe

girl

glass

go

"**Go** away, Goats!"

goose

grandfather

Your father's father or your mother's father.

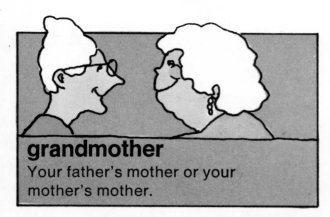

grandmother
Your father's mother or your mother's mother.

grass

grow
Flowers **grow**. So do people.

guess
Can you **guess** who is hiding behind this tree?

gun

h H

hair
Hairy Harry.

half
Harry wearing **half** of his hat.

hall
Harry in the **hall**.

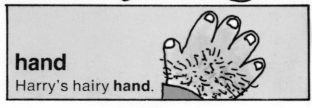

hammer

hand
Harry's hairy **hand**.

happy

Happy hairy Harry.

head

Hairy Harry's **head**.

heavy

Harry's horn is very **heavy**.

helicopter

hello

Hello Harry.

hen

hide
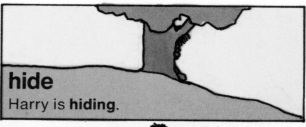
Harry is **hiding**.

high

Harry is **high** up on a hill.

hit

"**Hit** the ball!"

hole
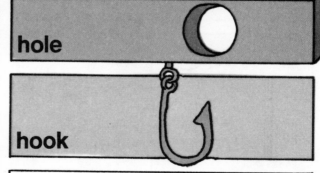

hook

hop

Harry **hopping**.

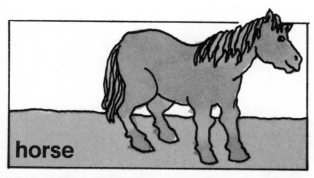

horse

hot

"This food is **hot!**"

house

hungry

Harry is still **hungry**.
The food is still too hot.

hurry

"**Hurry** home, Harry."

i I

ice

Frozen water.

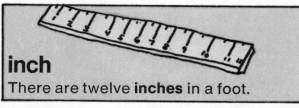

ice cream

igloo

This Eskimo lives in an **igloo**.

inch

There are twelve **inches** in a foot.

ink

Irving spilled the **ink**.

insect

A bug.

inside
Irving **inside** a box.

itch
Irving scratching an **itch**.

j J

jacket
Jack's **jacket**.

jack-in-the-box

jack-o'-lantern

jam
Jam in a **jam** jar.
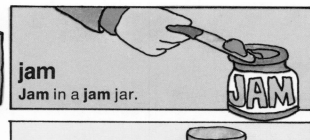

jelly
Jelly in a **jelly** jar.

juice
Jack drinking **juice**.

jump
Jack **jumping**.

junk

k K

kangaroo

keep
"Mom, can I **keep** the kangaroo?"

key

kick
A kangaroo **kicking** a ball.

king

kiss

kite
A kangaroo flying a **kite**.

knee
Two **knees**.

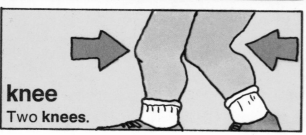

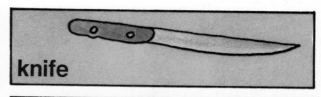

knife

knob
A **doorknob**.

I L

ladder

lamb
A baby sheep.

land
This plane **lands** on water.

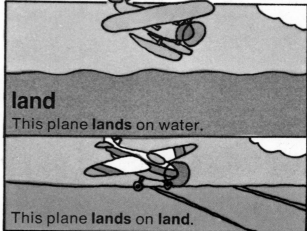

This plane **lands** on **land**.

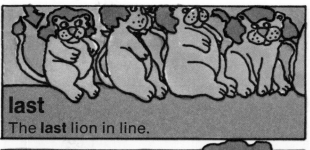

last
The **last** lion in line.

light
This **light** is lit.

laugh
A **laughing** lion. Ha-ha.

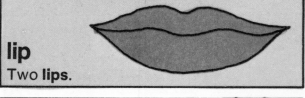

lip
Two **lips**.

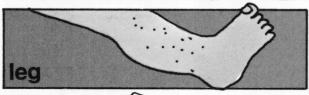

leg

little
A **little** lion.

letter

DEAR LION,
I THINK YOU
ARE VERY
FUNNY.
LOVE,
MAX MOOSE

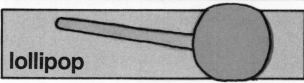

lollipop

library
A **library** is full of books.

look
A lion **looks** in his lunchbox.

PHEW!

lift
Lifting a lion is hard work.

love
Lions **love** lunch.

m M

machine
Max Moose made this **machine.**
It doesn't work.

magic
A **magician** doing **magic** tricks.

mail
A **mail** carrier delivers the **mail.**

man
One **man.**

many
Many men.

mask
Max Moose in a **mask.**

mess
A mouse in a **mess.**

monkey

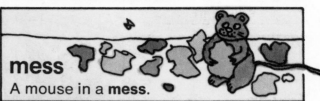

moon

morning
"Good **morning,** Max."

mother
Max's **mother,** Mrs. Moose.

more
More messy mice.

mouth

move
Mrs. Moose **moving**.

mud
Max in the **mud**.

music
A mouse making **music**.

n N

nail

name
My **name** is Norbert.

near
Norbert lives **near** a tree.

neck
Norbert's **neck**.

nest

new
Norbert's **new** necktie.

newspaper

night
"Good **night**, Norbert."

noodles
Norbert eating **noodles**.

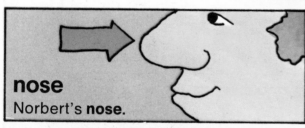

nose
Norbert's **nose**.

nothing
There is **nothing** in the box.

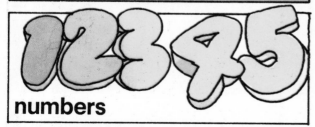

numbers

nut

o O

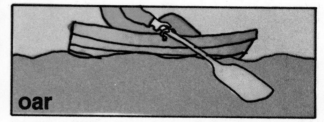

oar

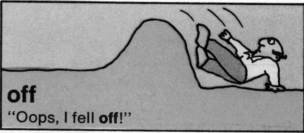

off
"Oops, I fell **off**!"

oil
Oil in an oilcan.

old
An **old** ostrich.

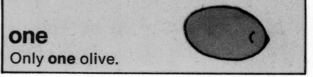

one
Only **one** olive.

open

The door is **open**.

orange
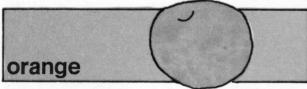

out

An old ostrich going **out** the door.

over

An owl **over** an ostrich.

overalls
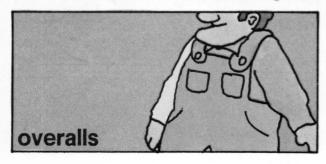

p P

pail

paint

A pig **painting**.

pair

A **pair** of pigs.

pajamas

A pig in **pajamas**.

pan
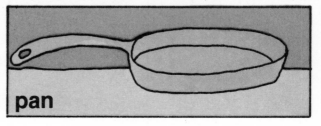

pants

parachute

party
Three pigs at a **party**.

peanut

pen

pencil

phone

pie

plant

plate

play
Pigs **playing** ball.

pocket
A pig's pants have **pockets**.

policeman

pot

potato

pretty
Peggy Pig is **pretty**.

pull
A pig **pulling** a penguin.

push
A pig **pushing** a penguin.

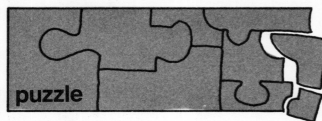

puzzle

q Q

quart
This is a **quart** of milk.

queen
This is a **queen**.

question
The Queen asks a **question**.
"How much milk is this?"

quick
"Answer the question **quickly**!"

quiet
"Be **quiet**, Queen, I'm sleeping."

r R

race
The rabbits are **racing**.

rain
The rabbits are racing in the **rain**.

raincoats
It's OK, the rabbits have **raincoats**.

read
This rabbit is **reading**.

rest
This rabbit is **resting**.

ride
These rabbits are **riding**.

ring

road

rocket

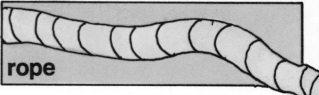

roof

rope

rose

saddle

round

Round things roll.

safe

Money is **safe** in a **safe**.

run

The rabbits are **running** again.

sail

A **sailor** is **sailing** his **sailboat**.
See the **sailboat's sail**.

s S

sandwich

sad

A **sad** sailor.

saw

The sailor **saw** a **saw**.

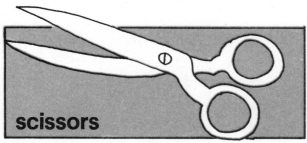

scissors

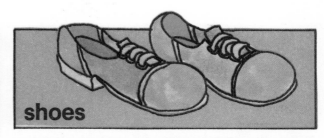

shoes

see

"I **see** a saw," the sailor said.

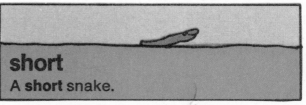

short

A **short** snake.

seven

Seven sailor hats.

shut

Shut the door.

shadow

sing

Sailors **singing**.

sharp

Some sticks are **sharp**.

sit

Sailors **sitting**.

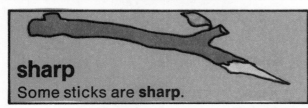

sheep

sleep

Sailors **sleeping**.

small
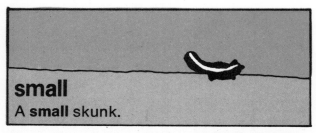
A **small** skunk.

swim

Sailors **swimming**.

smell

I **smell** a skunk.

t T

smile

table

snow

tail

A tiger's **tail**.

spots
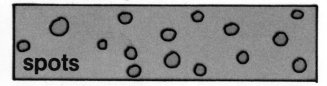

tall

A **tall** tiger.

straight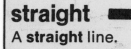
A **straight** line.

sun

tame

A **tame** tiger with a tiger **tamer**.

television

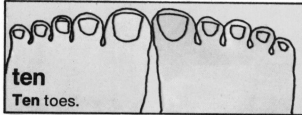
ten
Ten toes.

three
Three turtles.

throw
A tiger **throwing** a tiger tamer.

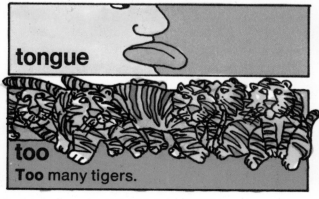
tongue

too
Too many tigers.

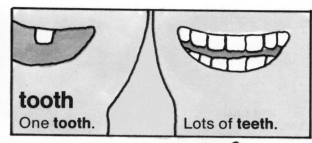
tooth
One **tooth**.   Lots of **teeth**.

top
A turtle on **top** of a tiger.

toy
A **toy** tiger.

train
A **train** on tracks.

tree

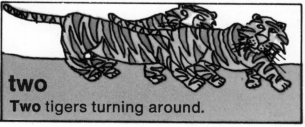
two
Two tigers turning around.

u U

umbrella
A man under an **umbrella**.

underwear
He is wearing his **underwear**!

up

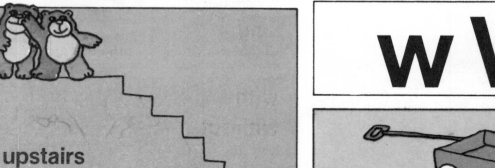

upstairs
The bears live **upstairs**.

v V

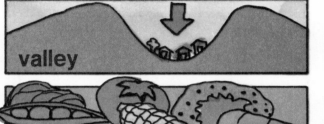

valley

vegetables

very
A **very** small elephant.

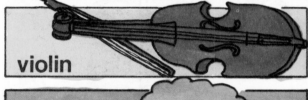

violin

volcano

w W

wagon

wait
"Hey, **wait** for me!"

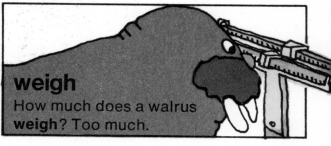

weigh
How much does a walrus **weigh**? Too much.

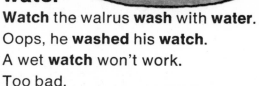

walk
A walrus **walking** away.

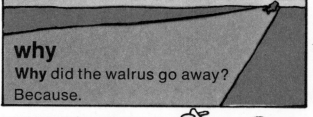

went
The walrus **went** away.

wash
watch
water
Watch the walrus **wash** with **water**.
Oops, he **washed** his **watch**.
A wet **watch** won't work.
Too bad.

wheel

whistle

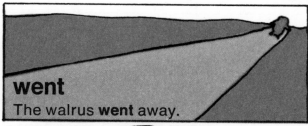

why
Why did the walrus go away?
Because.

wing
Birds have **wings**. So do airplanes.

wear
This walrus **wears** a white hat.

with
without
With a hat. **Without** a hat.

write
The walrus can **write**. Right?

wrong
The walrus can't write at all.

x X

x-ray
An **x/ray** is a picture of your insides.

xylophone

y Y

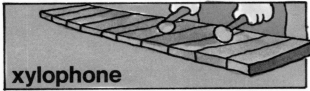

yard
There's a yak in my **yard**.

yawn

yell
The yak is **yelling**.

yes
Do you see the yak?
Yes, I do.

yo-yo

z Z

zebra

zipper

zoo
This book is finished.
Let's go to the **zoo**.

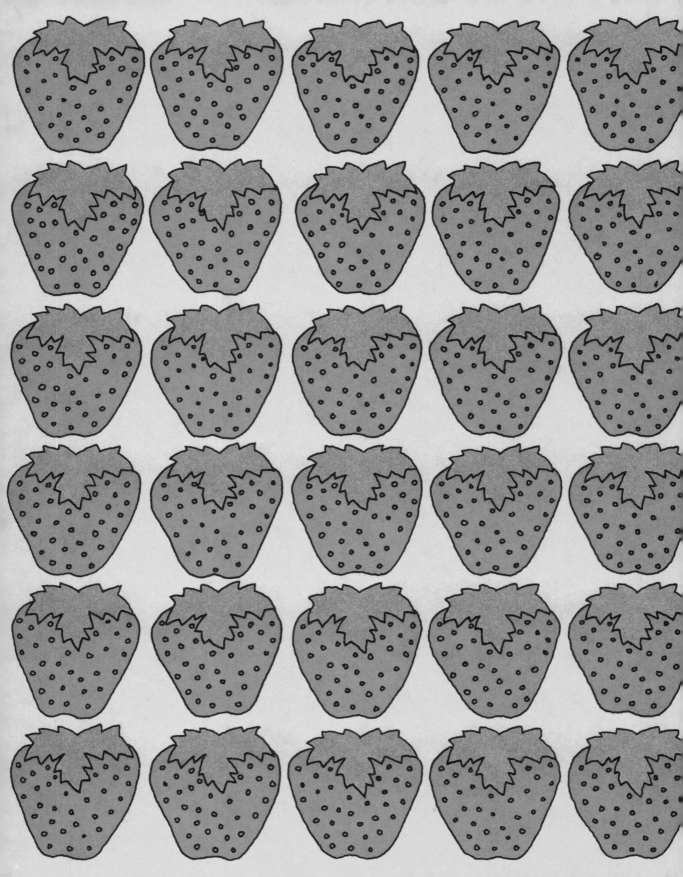